Warren Hastings

A Letter to the Court of Directors of the East-India Company

Warren Hastings

A Letter to the Court of Directors of the East-India Company

ISBN/EAN: 9783337013479

Printed in Europe, USA, Canada, Australia, Japan

Cover: Foto ©ninafisch / pixelio.de

More available books at **www.hansebooks.com**

A

LETTER

TO THE

Court of Directors

OF THE

EAST-INDIA COMPANY

FROM

WARREN HASTINGS, Esq.
Governor-General of Bengal.

Dated, Fort-William, March 20, 1783.

LONDON:

Printed for GEORGE ROBINSON, in
PATER-NOSTER ROW.
MDCCLXXXIII.

PREFACE.

THE following LETTER was read on the 23d inftant at a General Court of Proprietors. The gentlemen who were prefent wifhed it might be publifhed; to which there can be no objection, becaufe a copy if it lies at the India-Houfe for every body to perufe. For the better underftanding the Letter, it has been thought proper to print, from the Reports of the Select Committee, fuch parts of the Company's General Letter as are alluded to by Mr. Haftings.

London,
September 27, 1783.

EX-

EXTRACTS

FROM THE

GENERAL LETTER to BENGAL,

Dated the 28th of Auguft, 1782.

 OUR proceedings, refpecting Mr. Francis Fowke, are really furprifing to us. Mr. Fowke's firft appointment, to be Refident at Benaris, was in Auguft, 1775. He was recalled from thence in Auguft, 1776, and Mr. Graham appointed to fucceed him. —
Our

Our orders, however of the 30th of January, 1778, were positive for his restoration; but they were rendered ineffectual by your resolution, in July, 1778, to suspend the execution of them. In May, 1779, we repeated the orders respecting Mr. Fowke; and, in consequence thereof, Mr. Fowke was again appointed to proceed to Benaris. But judge of our astonishment, to find that, in January, 1781, in contempt of our authority, Mr. Fowke was once more removed from his station at Benaris. So far from a charge having been brought against him, on which ground alone his removal could be justified, we find his conduct approved and his character esteemed; and, in lieu of the station from which he is thus removed, another positive order of the Company was broken through, by his being appointed agent for the provision of boats to be employed for the military service of your establishment, with a commission of 15 per cent. upon his disbursements, and an allowance given him of rupees, 1000 per month, until the expiration of the then-subsisting contract.

Without

Without pretending to difapprove of the conduct of Mr. Markham, who was appointed to fucceed Mr. Fowke at Benaris, but merely to vindicate the authority of the Court of Directors, we hereby direct, that Mr. Fowke do immediately refume his ftation at Benaris. As to the boat-agency, that appointment muft be immediately annulled, and the bufinefs performed by contract, in the manner repeatedly laid down for your guidance.

Equally extraordinary and unwarrantable have been your proceedings refpecting Mr. John Briftow. He was appointed Refident at Owde, in December, 1774. In December, 1776, he was recalled, without the fhadow of a charge being exhibited againft him. By our letter, of the 4th of July, 1777, we fignified our difapprobation of the proceedings againft Mr. Briftow, and directed that he fhould be reftored to his ftation, which direction we confirmed by our fubfequent letter of the 23d of December, 1787.

1778. Mr. Briſtow arrived in India in February, 1780; and, in October in the ſame year, i was reſolved, by your Board, that Mr. Briſtow ſhould return to Owde, but that his appointment ſhould be limited ſolely to the conduct of political negociations, Mr. Middleton being, at the ſame time, nominated to ſettle pecuniary matters with the Vizier. On the 21ſt of May, 1781, upon receiving a letter from the Vizier, expreſſing a deſire that Mr. Briſtow ſhould be removed from his court, he was again recalled. But, without entering into the conſideration of this matter, and in order to vindicate our authority, — We do hereby poſitively direct, that Mr. Briſtow do forthwith proceed to Owde, in the ſtation of our Reſident there. We do not mean in the leaſt to reflect on the character and ability of Mr. Middleton, who muſt be immediately recalled from thence; but it is a duty incumbent on us thus to maintain the reſpect due to the orders of the Court of Directors. You are likewiſe to obſerve, that we ſhall not ſuffer any other perſon to proceed to Owde for the management of the finance; one perſon being, in our opinion, ſufficient to tranſact our buſineſs there, as principal in both
- departments;

departments; and we expect our orders, respecting the succession to that Residency, to be fully complied with,

---

The proceedings of your government, respecting Rajah Cheit Sing, have been, for some time, under our serious confideration. Our enquiry commenced with the death of Sujah Dowlah, in 1775; when the Governor-general and Council concluded a treaty with his succefsor, by which the Zemeendarry of Benaris, with its dependencies, was furrendered, in perpetuity, to the Company.

Previous to the conclufion of the beforementioned treaty, we find that, on the 13th of February, 1775, the Governor-general propofed, that each member of the Board fhould deliver in his fentiments of the conditions to be required or acceded to for the new treaty. This was accordingly done; and, on the opinions then delivered, the Governor-general propofed, that the perpetual and independent poffeffion of

the Zemeendarry of Benaris, and its dependencies, be confirmed and guaranteed to Rajah Cheit Sing and his heirs for ever; subject only to the annual payment of the revenue hitherto paid to the late Vizier, amounting to Benaris Sicca rupees 23,71,656 12; that no other demand be made upon him, either by the Nabob of Owde or your government; nor any kind of authority or jurisdiction exercised by either within the dominions assigned him. The Governor-general's observations on this proposition are as follow: " The Rajah of Benaris, from
" the situation of his country, which is a frontier
" both to the provinces of Owde and Bahar,
" may be made a serviceable ally to the Com-
" pany, whenever their affairs shall require it.
" He has always been considered in this light,
" both by the Company and the successive
" members of the late Council; but, to ensure
" his attachment to the Company, his interest
" must be connected with it, which cannot be
" better effected than by freeing him totally
" from the remains of his present vassalage un-
" der the guarantee and protection of the Com-
" pany, and, at the same time, guarding him
" against any apprehensions from this govern-
" ment,

" ment, by thus pledging its faith that no
" encroachments fhall be made on his rights by
" the Company."

On the 3d of March, the Board refume the
confideration of the bufinefs, and the Governor-
general propofes the following queftions: ——
" Whether it fhall be made a condition of the
" new treaty, that Rajah Cheit Sing fhall exer-
" cife a free and independent authority in his
" own dominions, fubject only to the payment
" of his tribute ?"
This queftion was refolved in the affirma-
tive.

Every preliminary being fettled with the Vizier, and the treaty executed, the Governor-
general, on the 12th of June, 1775, laid before the Board a minute, with obfervations,
refpecting the arrangements to be made with Rajah Cheit Sing, in which he declares his readi-
nefs to acquiefce in any plan which may be propofed, on terms by which more effectual provi-
fion may be made for the intereft of the Com-

pany,

pany, without an encroachment on the juſt
rights of the Rajah or the engagements actu-
ally ſubſiſting with him. He propoſes, that
Cheit Sing ſhall pay to the Company, in equal
monthly payments, the yearly revenue of
22,48,449 Sonaut rupees ; that he ſhall be em-
powered to exercife a complete and uncontrouled
authority over his Zemeendarry, under the ac-
knowledged ſovereignty of the Company ; that
he ſhall maintain, in conſtant pay, a body of
2000 horſe, for the ſervice of the Company,
whenever they ſhall be required ; and that,
while the Rajah ſhall continue faithful to theſe
engagements and punctual in his payments,
and ſhall pay due obedience to the authority of
your government, no more demands ſhall be
made upon him, by the Company, of any kind ;
nor, on any pretence whatſoever, ſhall any perfons be allowed to interfere with his authority,
or to diſturb the peace of his country. At the
concluſion of this Minute, the Governor-general
obſerves, " That voluntary reſtraint, made by
" the government on its own actions, will af-
" ford the Rajah the greateſt confidence ; and
" naturally inſpire him with ſentiments of fide-
" lity and attachmen", both from the principles
" of

" of gratitude and felf-intereft. Without fome
" fuch appearance, he will expect, with every
" change of government, additional demands
" to be made upon him ; and will, of courfe,
" defcend to all the arts of intrigue and con-
" cealment practifed by other dependent Rajahs,
" which will keep him indigent and weak, and
" eventually prove hurtful to the Company.
" By proper encouragement and protection, he
" may prove a profitable dependent, an ufeful
" barrier, and even a powerful ally, to the
" Company ; but he will be neither, if the
" conditions of his connection with the Com-
" pany, are left open to future variations." —
On the 5th of July, the Board agree with the
Governor-general, except in the article to *oblige*
Rajah Cheit Sing to keep up a body of 2000
horfe. They refolved, indeed, to recommend
the fame to him ; but declare there fhall be no
obligation on him to do it ; the Governor-general at the fame time obferving, that it was far
from his intention to propofe this or any other
article to be impofed on the Rajah by compul-
fion.

We

We are much furprifed at the conduct of the Governor-general towards the Rajah on his arrival at Benaris, when we obferve that, by the inftructions he received for his guidance, previous to his departure from Calcutta, the arrangements he was to make with Cheit Sing *were to be confonant to the mutual relation and actual engagements fubfifting between the Company and him.*

The imprifonment of his perfon in the midft of his country, which, for time immemorial, has been the refidence of the moft refpectable perfons of Hindoflan, thereby difgracing him in the eyes of his fubjects and others, was unwarrantable and highly impolitic, and may tend to weaken the confidence which the native princes of India ought to have in the juftice and moderation of the Company's government.

The

The refolutions of the Court of Directors, on your proceedings relative to Cheit Sing, are as follow :

" That it appears to this Court, that, on the
" death of Sujah Dowlah, 1775, a treaty
" was made by his fucceffor, by which
" the Zemeendarry of Benaris, and its
" dependencies, was ceded in perpetuity to
" the Company.

" That it appears to this Court, that Rajah
" Cheit Sing was confirmed, by the Go-
" vernor-general and Council of Bengal,
" in the management of the faid Zemeen-
" darry, (fubject to the fovereignty of
" the Company,) on his paying a certain
" tribute to the Company, which was
" fettled at Sicca rupees 22,66,180; and
" that the Bengal government pledged it-
" felf that the free and uncontrouled pof-
" feffion of the Zemeendarry of Benaris and
" its dependencies fhould be confirmed and
" guaranteed to the Rajah, and his heirs, for
" ever, fubject to fuch tribute ; and that no
" other demand fhould be made upon
" him,

" him, nor any kind of authority or jurif-
" diction exercifed within the dominions
" affigned him, fo long as he adhered to
" the terms of his engagements.

" That it appears to this Court, that the
" Governor-general and Council did, on
" the 5th of July, 1775, recommend to
" Rajah Cheit Sing to keep up a body of
" 2000 horfe; but at the fame time de-
" clared, there fhould be no obligation on
" him to do it.

" That it appears to this Court, that Rajah
" Cheit Sing performed his engagements
" with the Company, in the regular pay-
" ment of his tribute of Sicca rupees
" 22,66,180.

" That it appears to this Court, that the
" conduct of the Governor-general to-
" wards the Rajah, whilft he was at Be-
" naris, was improper; and that the im-
" prifonment of his perfon, thereby dif-
" gracing him in the eyes of his fubjects
" and others, was unwarrantable and
" highly impolitic, and may tend to
" weaken the confidence which the native
" princes of India ought to have in the
" juftice

" juftice and moderation of the Compa-
" ny's government."

Such farther refolutions, as we may think
proper to come to on this very important fubject, will be communicated to you by a future
conveyance; but we cannot avoid remarking,
that, by the Governor-general's laft Narrative,
the real object of his journey to Benaris was to
exact from Cheit Sing 40 or 50 lacks of rupees,
or to remove him from his Zemeendarry, as appears by a confidential converfation, which paffed between the Governor-general and Mr.
Wheler (as ftated in the Narrative) previous to
the Governor-general's departure.

N. B. The letter, from which the foregoing
extracts were taken, was figned by the two
Chairs and eleven Directors.

C

T

TO THE HONOURABLE

COURT of DIRECTORS

OF THE HONOURABLE

United EAST-INDIA COMPANY,

FORT-WILLIAM, 20th March, 1783.

Honourable Sirs,

I N your letter to the Governor-general and Council, dated the 28th of Auguſt, 1782, you have been pleaſed to enter into a large diſcuſſion of my proceedings at Benaris, and to appriſe the Board of certain reſolutions, comprehending your judgement upon them. Theſe reſolutions, as the immediate cauſe and ſubject of my preſent addreſs, I ſhall, to avoid the perplexity of frequent and remote reference, hereto ſubjoin:

C 2 " That

" That it appears to this Court, that, on
" the death of Sujah Dowlah, 1775, a
" treaty was made with his fucceffor, by
" which the Zemeendarry of Benaris, with
" its dependencies, was ceded in perpe-
" tuity to the Eaft-India Company.

That it appears to this Court, that Rajah
" Cheyt Sing was confirmed by the Go-
" vernor-general and the Council of Ben-
" gal in the management of the faid Ze-
" mindarry, (fubject to the fovereignty of
" the Company,) on his paying a certain
" tribute, which was fettled at Sicca ru-
" pees 22,66,180; and that the Bengal
" Government pledged itfelf, that the free
" and uncontrouled poffeffion of the Ze-
" mindarry of Benaris, and its dependen-
" cies, fhould be confirmed and guaran-
" teed to the Rajah and his heirs for ever,
" fubject to fuch tribute; and that no o-
" ther demand fhould be made upon him,
" nor any kind of authority or jurifdiction
" exercifed within the dominions affigned
" him, fo long as he adhered to the terms
" of his engagements.

" That

" That it appears to this Court, that the
" Governor-general and Council did, on
" the 5th of July, 1775, recommend to
" Rajah Cheyt Sing to keep up a body of
" 2000 horse; but at the same time de-
" clared there should be no obligation on
" him to do it.

" That it appears to this Court, that Rajah
" Cheyt Sing performed his engagements
" with the Company, in the regular pay-
" ment of his tribute of Sicca rupees
" 22,66,180.

" That it appears to this Court, that the
" conduct of the Governor-general to-
" wards the Rajah whilst he was at Be-
" naris was improper, and that the im-
" prisonment of his person, thereby dif-
" gracing him in the eyes of his subjects
" and others, was unwarrantable and high-
" ly impolitic, and may tend to weaken
" the confidence which the native princes
" of India ought to have in the justice
" and moderation of the Company's go-
" vernment."

I understand that these resolutions were either
published or intended for publication. As they
have proceeded from an authority so respect-

able, every reader of them will naturally and without hesitation believe, that the facts, on which they necessarily and indispensably depend, have been fully established. And who are the readers? not the proprietors alone, whose interest is immediately concerned in them, and whose approbation I am impelled, by every motive of pride and gratitude, to solicit; but the whole body of the people of England; whose passions have been excited on the general subject of the conduct of their servants in India; and before them I am arraigned and prejudged of a violation of the national faith in acts of such complicated aggravation, that, if they were true, no punishment, short of death, could atone for the injury which the interest and credit of the public had sustained in them:

I hope, therefore, I shall not be thought to give unnecessary trouble in calling your attention to a subject not wholly personal, nor to fail in the respect, in which I have never yet failed, to your Honourable Court, in the mode of my vindication, which will not admit of the common delicacies of expression; for I cannot admit facts, however affirmed, which I know to have no existence, and by which my character

ter

ter has been blasted; nor will a simple denial
or refutation of them be sufficient against such
a charge, if I can at the same time appeal to
your own knowledge, proved by the evidence
of your own arguments, and to what your Honourable Court possesses of candour for my first
justification and acquittal.

The facts affirmed, or expressed in terms
equal to affirmation, in your resolutions, are as
follow: ——

I. That the Bengal Government pledged itself, that the free and uncontrouled possession
of the Zemindarry of Benaris, and its dependencies, should be confirmed and guaranteed to
the Rajah and his heirs for ever.

II. That it pledged itself that no other demand should be made upon him, nor any kind
of authority or jurisdiction exercised within his
dominions assigned him, so long as he adhered
to the terms of his engagements.

III. That the Governor-general required
him to keep up a body of 2000 horse, contrary
to the declaration made to him by the Governor-
general and Council on the 5th of July, 1775,

that there fhould be no obligation on him to do it.

IV. That Rajah Cheyt Sing was bound by no other engagements to the Company than for the payment of his tribute of Sicca rupees 22,66,180.

V. That Rajah Cheyt Sing was a native prince of India.

The judgement paffed on my conduct, as deducible from thefe facts, is, that it was " improper, unwarrantable, and highly impo- " litic, and may tend to weaken the confi- " dence which the native princes of India " ought to have in the juftice and moderation " of the Company's Government." Here I muft crave leave to fay, that the terms " im- " proper, unwarrantable, and highly impoli- " tic," are much too gentle as deductions from fuch premifes ; and, as every reader of the let- ter will obvioufly feel as he reads the deduc- tions which inevitably belong to them, I will add, that the ftrict performance of folemn en- gagements on one part, followed by acts direct- ly fubverfive of them, and by total difpoffef- fion on the other, ftamps on the perpetrators

of

of the letter, the guilt of the greateft poffible violation of faith and juftice.

But this, and every other conclufion from the facts adduced in proof of them will fall, if the facts themfelves have no exiftence. I do therefore moft pofitively and folemnly deny their exiftence.

I deny that the Bengal government pledged itfelf, that the free and uncontrouled poffeffion of the Zemindarry of Benaris and its dependencies fhould be confirmed and guaranteed to the Rajah and his heirs for ever.

I deny that the Bengal government pledged itfelf that no other demand fhould be made upon him, nor any kind of authority or jurifdiction exercifed within the dominions affigned him, fo long as he adhered to the terms of his engagements.

I deny that I ever required him to keep up a body of 2000 horfe, contrary to the declaration made to him by the Governor-general and Council on the 5th of July, 1775, that there fhould be no obligation on him to do it.

My demand, that is, the demand of the Board, was not that he fhould maintain any fpecific number of horfe; but that the number

D   which

which he did maintain fhould be employed for the defence of the general State. '

I deny that Rajah Cheyt Sing was bound by no other engagements to the Company, than for the payment of his tribute of Sicca rupees 22,66,180.

He was bound by the engagements of fealty, and of abfolute obedience to every order of the government which he ferved. The various and repeated profeffions of his letters are proofs and acknowledgments of this conftruction of his vaffalage; and his own cabuleeat, or the inftrument by which he engaged to perform the duties of his Zemindarry, expreffes it in the acknowledgment of the Company's fovereignty.

I deny that Rajah Cheyt Sing was a native prince of India.

Cheyt Sing is the fon of a collector of the revenue of that province, which his arts, and the misfortunes of his mafter, enabled him to convert to a permanent and hereditary poffeffion. This man, whom you have thus ranked amongft the princes of India, will be aftonifhed, when he hears it, at an elevation fo unlooked-for, nor lefs at the independent rights which your commands have affigned him; rights which are fo

foreign

foreign from his conceptions, that I doubt whether he will know in what language to af-fert them, unlefs the example which you have thought it confiftent with juftice, however op-pofite to policy, to fhew, of becoming his advocates againft your own interefts, fhould infpire any of your own fervants to be his advifers and inftructors.

I forbear to detail the proofs of thefe denials. In legal propriety I might perhaps claim a difpenfation from it, and require the charges to be proved, not myfelf difprove them. But I have already difproved them in my narrative of my proceedings at Benaris, which has been long fince in your hands, and is, I hope, in the hands of the public. To that I think it fufficient to refer, and to point out the ninth and following pages of the copy, which was printed in Calcutta, for a .complete explana-tion ; and I prefume as complete a demonftra-tion of the mutual relation of Rajah Cheyt Sing, the vaffal and fubject of the Company, and of the Company his fovereign.

The fubject to which I now proceed, and on which I reft my fulleft acquittal, is too de-licate to admit of my entering upon it without

requefting

requesting your indulgence and pardon for whatever may appear offensive in it, and declaring, that I should have submitted in silence to the severest expressions of censure which you could pass upon me, had they been no more than expressions, and applied to real facts; but, where the censures are not applied to real facts, and are such as substantially affect my moral character, I should be myself an accomplice in the injury, if I suffered the slightest imputation to remain, which it was in my power wholly to efface.

A breach of faith necessarily implies antecedent and existing engagements, and can only be construed such by the express terms of those engagements. I have been guilty of this crime in my treatment of Cheyt Sing, or of none; and I may be allowed to regret, that, while you stated such facts as implied it, you did not in terms declare it. There is an appearance of tenderness in this deviation from plain construction, of which, however meant, I have a right to complain, because it imposes on me the necessity of framing the terms of the accusation against myself, which you have not only made, but have stated the leading argument to it so
strongly,

ftrongly, that no one, who reads thefe, can avoid making it, or not know to have been intended.

But, permit me to afk, May I not prefume that this deviation arpfe from fomething more than a tendernefs for my character or feelings? that it was dictated by a conciqufnefs that no fuch engagements exifted? For, if any fuch did exift, why were they not produced in fupport of the charges?

Even the facts, which are affirmed in the refolutions, are fuch as muft depend upon fome evidence, for they cannot exift independently. If the Bengal government " pledged itfelf," its pledge muft be contained in the written inftruments which were exprefsly formed, and declared to define the reciprocal relation and obligation of the Rajah and the Company.

The refolutions of your honourable Court, as they ftand unconnected in their original ftate, muft be accepted as the conclufions from certain and eftablifhed evidence; and this evidence, I muft prefume, you meant to produce in the long procefs of detailed argument which precedes them in your general letter. This confifts of pieced extracts, from opinions delivered by me in the debates of Council, which

which not only preceded the fettlement, made with the Rajah Cheyt Sing, when his Zemindarry became the property of the Company; but, ftrange as it will appear, which paffed on an occafion wholly foreign from it, and at a time when the Company had, not obtained the ceffion of the Zemindarry. At the point of the fettlement your detail ftops. Had it proceeded, it muft have exhibited the conditions of the fettlement, which would have contradicted every fact which you have afferted; and every man of candour will believe that this was the only reafon why it did not proceed. For why are my fpeculative opinions on the claim made upon the Nabob Affof ul Dowlah at the ceffion of the Zemindarry of Benaris, which I thought an infringement of a treaty already fubfifting with him; and upon the mode by which we fhould allow Rajah Cheyt Sing to exercife the management of his Zemindarry, when it had become the property of the Company, quoted in evidence againft me; when the actual deeds which conveyed to Cheyt Sing his poffeffion of the Zemindarry, and all the conditions on which he held it, were the only criteria by which my conduct towards him could be tried? The de-

bates from which my opinions are extracted, are
so voluminous, and my share in them bears so
large a proportion, that it would take up much
time and argument to prove, what I could
prove, that in their collective and relative sense
they are perfectly consistent, so far as they can
apply at all to my subsequent conduct; but,
were it otherwise, they were not to be made
the rules of my conduct; and God forbid that
every expression dictated by the impulse of
present emergency, and unpremeditatedly ut-
tered in the heat of party contention, should
impose upon me the obligation of a fixed principle, and be applied to every variable occasion.

The wisdom of the Legislature has declared,
that the whole collective body of the Governor-
general and Council shall be bound by the opinions of the majority; but the doctrine implied
in your quotation of my opinions is the reverse
of that obligation, if my opinions were not con-
formable to those of a majority of the Board;
and, if they were, the acts of the Board, formed
on such concurrent opinions ought to be quoted as the rules of my conduct, not the opinions which only led to them.

Having

Having folemnly pronounced that Rajah Cheyt Sing had performed his engagements with the Company, and that my conduct towards him was " improper and unwarrantable," you proceed to fay, that " fuch farther refo- " folutions, as you may think proper to come " to on this very important fubject, will be " communicated to us by a future conveyance." This I cannot otherwife underftand than as an indication of your intention to order the reftoration of Rajah Cheyt Sing to the Zemindarry of Benaris. It will be expected, after the judgement which you have paffed, as an act of indifpenfable juftice; and, wheneverthis promiffory declaration is made public, as it muft be, if not already known, what may have been expected will be regarded as a certainty. If any thing were wanting but the exprefs notification of your intention to confirm it, the recall of Mr Markham, who was known to be the public agent of my own nomination at Benaris, and the re-appointment of Mr Francis Fowke by your order contained in the fame letter, would place it beyond a doubt. This order has been obeyed; and, whenever you fhall be pleafed to order the reftoration of Cheyt Sing,

I will

I will venture to promise the same ready and exact submission in the other members of your Council.

Of the consequences of such a policy I forbear to speak. Most happily the wretch, whose hopes may be excited by the appearances in his favour, is ill-qualified to avail himself of them ; and the force which is stationed in the province of Benaris is sufficient to suppress any symptoms of internal sedition : but it cannot fail to create distrust and suspense in the minds both of the rulers and of the people, and such a state is always productive of disorder.

But it is not in this partial consideration that I dread the effects of your commands. It is in your proclaimed indisposition against the first executive member of your first government in India. It is as well known to the Indian world as to the Court of English Proprietors, that the first declaratory instruments of the dissolution of my influence, in the year 1774, were Mr. John Bristow and Mr. Francis Fowke. By your ancient and known constitution the governor has been ever held forth and understood to possess the oftensible powers of government. All the correspondence with foreign princes is conduc-

E   ted

ted in his name ; and every perfon, refident with
them for the management of your political con-
cerns, is underftood to be more efpecially his
reprefentative, and of his choice: and fuch
ought to be the rule ; for how otherwife can,
they truft an agent nominated againft the will
of his principal; or how, knowing him to act
under the variable inftructions of a temporary
influence, or the cafual dictates of a majority,
can they rely on the meafures which he may
propofe, and which a fudden change of influence, always expected in a deviation from con-
ftitutional forms, may undo, and fubject them,
in every inftance of their connection, to a con-
tinual fluctuation of affairs ?

When the ftate of this adminiftration was
fuch as feemed to admit of the appointment of
Mr. Briftow to the refidency of Lucknow,
without much diminution of my own influence,
I gladly feized the occafion to fhew my readi-
nefs to fubmit to your commands. I propofed his nomination: he was nominated, and
declared to be the agent of my own choice.
Even this effect of my caution is defeated by
your abfolute command for his re-appointment,
independent of me, and with the fuppofition

that

that I fhould be adverfe to it. I am now wholly deprived of my official powers, both in the
Province of Owd and in the Zemindarry of Benaris.

Nor will the evil ftop at thefe lines. My
general influence, the effects of which have
been happily manifefted for the fupport of your
interefts, is now wholly loft, or what may remain of it fuftained only by the prefcription of
long pufieffion, and fomething perhaps of perfonal attachment, impreffed by the habits of
frequent intercourfe.

I almoft fhudder at the reflection of what
might have have happened, had thefe denun-
ciations, againft your own minifter, in favour
of a man univerfally confidered · in this part of
the world as juftly attainted for his crimes, the
murderer of your fervants and foldiers, and the
rebel to your authority, arrived two months
earlier. You will learn, by our common dif-
patches, what difficulties Mahdajee Sindia has
had to furmount in reconciling the different
members of the Maratta ftate to the ratification,
and even, when ratified, to the interchange of
the treaty, concluded by him in May laft, with
this government. I dare to appeal even to your

judgement

judgement for the reply, and to aſk, whether the miniſters of the Peſhwa, poſſeſſing the know-ledge of ſuch a circumſtance, would not have availed themſelves of it to withhold their con-ſent to the treaty, either claiming to include Cheit Sing as a party in it, or either overtly or ſecretly ſupporting his pretenſions, with the view of multiplying our difficulties; or, which is moſt probable, waiting for the event of that change in the ſuperior government of Bengal, which ſuch ſymptoms portended, before they precipitated their intereſts in a connection with a declining influence, which they might ob-viouſly conclude would render this, with all its other acts, obnoxious to that which ſucceed-ed it.

Their counterpart of the treaty is ratified, and in our actual poſſeſſion; and, ſuch is the cha-racter of the man whom we have made our principal and the guarantee of it, that it will in-ſure us againſt any change of ſentiment, which might ariſe, from any cauſe, in the breaſts of his countrymen. I am happy in having been the ſole inſtrument of the accompliſhment of ſo great an event. It originated in a ſcene of univerſal revolt encompaſſing my own perſon: it began

with the immediate feparation of the firft power of the Maratta ftate from the general war,
and was followed by the inftant and general
ceffation of hoftilities; in effect, by a permanent peace; for I have a right now to affirm
this, having pofitively affured you that it would
prove fuch, while the formal confirmation of it
remained fo long in a ftate of fufpenfe. In
every progreffive ftate of it, it has met with
obftructions which might have difcouraged
even the moft determined perfeverance; in the
known indifpofition of the prefidency of Bom-
bay; in the calamities of the Carnatic; in the
alarming interference of the Prefident and Select Committee of Fort St. George, by the ex-
aggerated portrait of their affairs in a letter ad-
dreffed to our minifter, and fent in circulation
th ough the midft of Deccan and Indoftan,
intreating him at all events, and with whatever
facrifices, to precipitate the conclufion of the
treaty, and fave them from deftruction; but,
above all, in the vehement exclamations for
peace from men of every defcription in Great-
Britain. To all thefe counteractions I have
oppofed the principle of firmnefs and defiance;
and, aided by the peculiar talents, and warinefs,
and

and incomparable perfeverance, of Mr. David
Anderfon, I have at length brought my wifhes
and yours to their deftined point. Perhaps with
a lefs able minifter I might yet have failed ; but
even the merits of his fervices I claim as my
own; for it was my choice which called his
mind into action, and my confidence that gave
it its beft exertion. Padon, honourable Sirs,
this digreffive exultation. I cannot fupprefs
the pride which I feel in this fuccefsful atchieve-
ment of a meafure fo fortunate for your interefts and the national honour; for that pride
is the fource of my zeal fo frequently exerted in
your fupport, and never more happily than in
thofe inftances in which I have departed from
the prefcribed and beaten path of action, and
affumed a refponfibility which has too frequently
drawn on me the moft pointed effects of your
difpleafure. But, however I may yield to my
private feelings in thus enlarging on the fubject,
my motive in introducing it was immediately
connected with its context, and was to contraft
the actual ftate of your political affairs derived
from a happier influence with that which might
have attended an earlier diffolution of it.

It

It is now a complete period of eleven years since I firſt received the nominal charge of your affairs. In the courſe of it I have invariably had to contend, not with ordinary difficulties, but ſuch as moſt unnaturally aroſe from the oppoſition of thoſe very powers from which I primarily derived my authority, and which were required for the ſupport of it. My exertions, though applied to an unvaried and confiſtent line of action, have been occaſional and deſultory : yet I pleaſe myſelf with the hope that, in the annals of your dominion which ſhall be written after the extinction of recent prejudices, this term of its adminiſtration will appear not the leaſt conducive to the intereſt of the Company, nor the leaſt reflective of the honour of the Britiſh name; and allow me to ſuggeſt the inſtructive reflection of what good might have been done, and what evil prevented, had due ſupport been given to that adminiſtration which has performed ſuch eminent and ſubſtantial ſervices without it.

. You, honourable Sirs, can atteſt the patience and temper with which I have ſubmitted to all the indignities which have been heaped upon me in this long ſervice. It was the duty of fideli-

ty

ty which I effentially owed to it; it was the return of gratitude which I owed, even with the
facrifice of life, had that been exacted, to
the Company, my original mafters and moft
indulgent patrons. To thefe principles have I
devoted every private feeling, and perfevered
in the violent maintenance of my office; becaufe I was confcious that I poffeffed, in my in-
tegrity, and in the advantags of local know-
ledge, thofe means of difcharging the functions
of it with credit to myfelf, and with advantage
to my employers, which might be wanting in
more fplendid talents ; and becaufe I had always
a ground of hope that my long fufferance would
difarm the prejudices of my adverfaries, or the
rotation of time produce that concurrence,
in the crifis of your fortune with my own, which
might place me in the fituation to which I af-
pired. In the mean time there was nothing in
any actual ftate of your affairs which could dif-
courage me from the profecution of this plan.
There was indeed an interval, and that of fome
duration, in which my authority was wholly
deftroyed; but another was fubftituted in its
place, and that, though irregular, was armed
with the public belief of an influence invifibly
upholding

upholding it, which gave it a vigour scarce less effectual than that of a constitutional power. Besides, your government had no external dangers to agitate, and discover the looseness of its composition.

The case is now most widely different. —— While your existence was threatened by wars with the most formidable powers of Europe, added to your Indian enemies; and while you confessedly owed its preservation to the seasonable and vigorous exertions of this government; you chose that season to annihilate its constitutional powers. You annihilated the influence of its executive member;——you proclaimed its annihilation; —— you virtually called on his associates to withdraw their support from him, and they have withdrawn it. But you have substituted no other instrument of rule in his stead, unless you suppose that it may exist, and can be effectually exercised, in the body of your Council at large; possessing no power of motion but an inert submission to the letter of your commands; which, however necessary in the wise intention of the legislature, have never yet been applied to the establishment of any original plan or system of measures, and seldom

F   felt

felt but in inftances of perfonal favour or perfonal difpleafure.

Under fuch a fituation, I feel myfelf impelled, by the fame fpirit which has hitherto
animated me to retain my poft againft all the at-
tempts made to extrude me from it, to adopt
the contrary line. The feafon for contention is
paft. The prefent ftate of affairs is not able to
bear it. I am morally certain, that my fucceffor in this government, whoever he may be,
will be allowed to poffefs and exercife the necef-
fary powers of his ftation, with the confidence
and fupport of thofe, who, by their choice of
him, will be interefted in his fuccefs. I am become a burthen to the fervice; and would inftantly relieve it from the incumbrance, were I
not apprehenfive of creating worfe confequences
by my abrupt removal from it. Such an act
would probably be confidered, by Mahdajee
Sindia, as a defertion of him in the inftant of
his accomplifhment of the treaty, and defeat
the purpofes of it, which remain yet to be effected by his agency. I am alfo perfuaded that
it would be attended with the lofs of the com-
mander in chief, in whofe prefence alone I look
for the reftoration of [peace to the Carnatic,

which

which he, perhaps, would think too hazardous an undertaking with no other fupport than that of a broken government. I have now no wifh remaining but to fee the clofe of this calamitous fcene, and for that I hope a few months will be fufficient. My fervices may afterwards be fafely withdrawn; but will ftill be due, in my conception of what I owe to my firft conftituents, until they can be regularly fupplied by thofe of my appointed fucceffor, or until his fucceffion fhall have been made known, and the interval but fhort for his arrival.

It therefore remains to perform the duty which I had affigned to myfelf as the final purpofe of this letter; to declare, as I now moft formally do, that it is my defire that you will be pleafed to obtain the early nomination of a perfon to fucceed me in the government of Fort William; to declare that it is my intention to refign your fervice as foon as I can do it without prejudice to your affairs, after the allowance of a competent time for your choice of a perfon to fucceed me; and to declare, that if, in the intermediate time, you fhall proceed to order the reftoration of Rajah Cheit Sing to the Zemeendarry, from which, by the powers I legally poffeffed, and

conceive

conceive myfelf legally bound to affert, againft any fubfequent authority to the contrary derived from the fame common fource, he was difpof-feffed for crimes of the greateft enormity, and your Council fhall refolve to execute the order; I will inftantly give up my ftation and the fervice.

To thefe declarations fuffer me to add this refervation: that if, in the mean time, the acts, of which I complain, fhall, on a mature revifion of them, be revoked, and I fhall find myfelf poffeffed of, fuch a degree of your confidence as fhall enable me to fupport the duties of my ftation, I will continue in it until the peace of all your poffeffions fhall be reftored, or it fhall be your pleafure to allow me to refign it.

I have the honour to be,

Honourable firs,

Your moft obedient

and faithful fervant,

WARREN HASTINGS.

P. S. Upon a careful revifal of what I have written, I fear that an expreffion, which I have ufed refpecting the probable conduct of the Board,

Board, in the event of orders being received for
the reftoration of Cheit Sing, may be conftrued
as intimating a fenfe of diffatisfaction applied to
tranfactions already paft. It is not my intention to complain of any one; but to vindicate
my own character, and to ftate the difficulties of
my fituation. Neither do I mean, by except-
ing one perfon, to caft a cenfure on any others.
Yet I feel, in my efteem for Mr. Wheler, and
in my folicitude to avoid even the imputation of
reflecting unjuftly on his conduct, a duty im-
pelling me to declare, that, in my experience
of it, fince the time that we were firft in the
habits of mutual confidence, it has been fair
and honourable to myfelf, and zealous to the
public; equally free from profeffion and fub-
terfuge, and his fupport, given to me in every
inftance, equal to whatever claim I might have
to it.

When Mr. Haftings wrote the preceding
letter, no account had been received, in Bengal,
of the very honourable and effectual fupport,
which ten gentlemen in the direction, and 428
proprietors, had given him, in oppofition to

13

ı3 directors and 75 proprietors, who voted to remove him for acts which did not originate with him. The Secretary of State forbade the Directors to fend intelligence of this event to India above ten months ago, nor has it been officially tranfmitted to this moment.

Mr. Haftings has always declared, that He would not abdicate, or run away from, his government, while it was under the preffure of fo great difficulties and fuch imminent dangers; but he would continue no longer than until he faw the Company fafe, and peace and tranquillity reftored. Great progrefs was made in this defirable work when his letter was written. Tippoo Saib evacuated Arcot on the 13th of March; and, on the fame day, our troops took poffeffion of the place. He has fince entirely quitted the Carnatic. Sir Eyre Coote left Bengal, the 23d of March, with ten lacks of rupees and a reinforcement of European artillery. The Maratta peace was finally and fully fettled, and fome progrefs made in a treaty of alliance with the Marattas, which would, in its confequences, effectually deftroy the power of Tippoo Saib. The provinces of Bengal, Bahar, Benaris, and Owde, were in perfect tranquillity.

The

The revenues increasing; and the salt-revenue, from a scheme solely owing to Mr. Haftings, has increased to fifty-seven lack of rupees per annum. Very confiderable retrenchments had been made in every branch of the public expenditure, and farther savings were about to take place. These great and important services were performed before there was any idea, in India, of a peace in Europe; and at a time, too, when, by the tenor of the Company's letters and the parliamentary proceedings, a diffolution of the government of Bengal appeared to be near. " What might have been done, " and what evil prevented, had due support " been given to that administration, which has " performed such eminent and substantial ser- " vices without it !"

T H E   E N D.